The Ar[illegible]
Resolving Problems

By Marilyn Brown
and Eileen Babcock

Illustrated by Karen Neulinger

ISBN 0-910857-69-5

EDUCATIONAL IMPRESSIONS, INC.
Hawthorne, NJ 07507

Table of Contents

To Acknowledge the Trailblazers

Solving problems and solving problems creatively are two different things. **Solving problems** may mean using only reason or logic to reach correct solutions. **Solving problems creatively** adds the limitless dimension of CREATIVITY and calls upon human beings to go through many processes to find the most appropriate solutions to well-defined problems.

It is with gratitude that the authors thank the following pioneers in the seeking and finding of those creative behaviors that make problem solving infinitely better:

Dr. E. Paul Torrance and J. Pansy Torrance
Researchers into creative behavior and developers of the Future Problem Solving Bowl for students.

Dr. J.P. Guilford
Researcher into the nature of creative intelligence.

Dr. Frank Williams
Developer of methods to encourage creative potential through the combination of thinking and feeling.

Dr. Sidney Parnes and Bea Parnes
Nurturers and developers of the Creative Problem Solving Institute.

These dedicated individuals continue to bring together the research in creativity and problem solving which keeps the creative spirit alive in all of us.

To the Adventurers Along the Trail

This book is designed to present teachers and students with the necessary methods for creative problem solving. The major elements of the creative and problem-solving techniques are sequentially developed to make acquiring these skills easier for teachers and students alike.

It is suggested that you follow the sequential order listed in the TABLE OF CONTENTS:

Path to Action (Creative Attitudes toward Solving Problems)
Base Camp Set-Ups (Prepare for Problem Solving)
Discoverer's Outlook (Identify the REAL Problem)
Inventive Leap (Creative Ideas for Alternative Solutions)
Mountain "Do" Cliffhangers (Implement Creative Solutions)

The COVER DESIGN presents a graphic picture of this same sequential problem-solving process. There are other graphic designs of the major processes of creative problem solving throughout the book.

The STUDENT PAGES are organized to...

- give the student a motto that reveals the intent or purpose of the page.
- motivate the student by explaining, just below the page title, a technique of creative problem solving.
- give an activity for the student to use to acquire a specific problem-solving skill.
- present at the bottom of the page a challenge which is intended to stretch the student's ability to deal with problems.

The ANIMALS illustrating the book may be used as memory links to the steps in the process of solving problems creatively.

The PROBLEM PEAKS present *safe* problems for students to resolve. As students become more familiar with the process, application to **real life problems** is essential.

The DISCUSSION REVIEW provides teachers with ideas for discussion after the lesson on the student page is completed. If students talk about the process of solving problems as they learn it, their understanding of that process will increase.

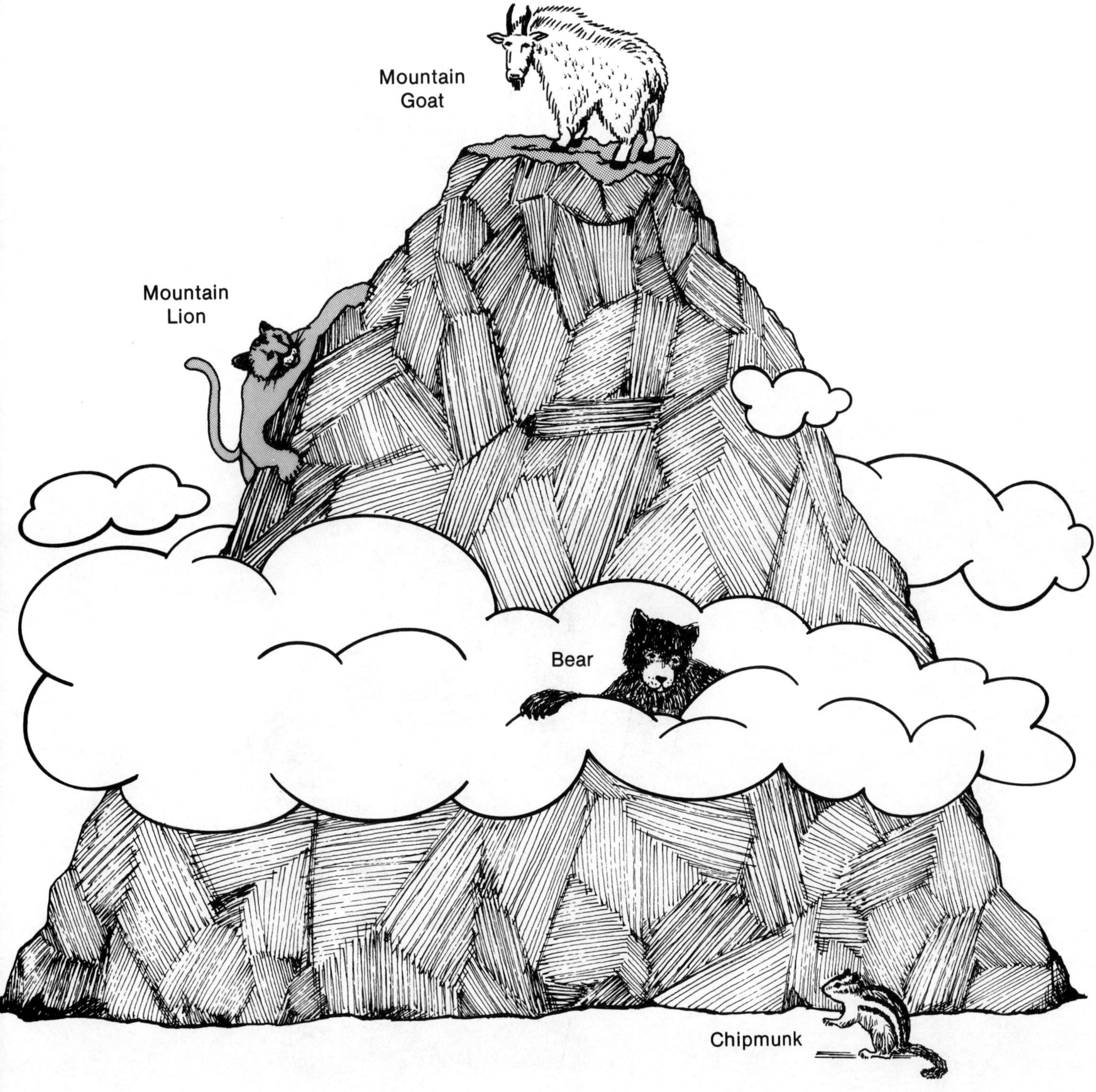
Mountain
Goat
Mountain
Lion
Bear
Chipmunk

SEARCH!

Path To Action

Creative Attitudes Toward Solving Problems

Teacher's Trail

Path to Action

Developing Creative Attitudes Toward Solving Problems:

Students who are in the fourth through sixth grades are very receptive and ready to develop their talents for the creative process. They are enthusiastic towards new ideas and have open attitudes. Research shows that the creative skills acquired during these grades—skills that are essential for the generation of creative solutions to problems—remain with the students throughout their school careers.

Suggested Teaching Routes:

1. The teacher should go over the student pages orally with the students BEFORE they do them.

2. Some of the pages are more effective when done in groups (teams) of three or four people. The teacher should decide which may be done alone and which provide a better understanding of the creative problem-solving process when done in groups.

3. Time should be taken to form groups of teams based on the following criteria:
   - A. Friends need not work together. (Sometimes children are inhibited by their friends.)
   - B. Balance the groups with different types of attitudes and personalities. (This adds fresh ideas and motivation to a group.)
   - C. Ideas must be RECORDED. (Creative people jot down their ideas so they won't forget them.)
     - Each group should select a recorder. You may have a different recorder for each problem.
     - The recorder should be able to jot down the main idea of a team member's suggestion.
     - Members of the team should take turns giving ideas so the recorder can write them down.
     - The recorder should take turns giving ideas too.
   - D. Remind students that there is no ownership of ideas. They create and give away their ideas to their team when they work on a problem.

4. The teacher should set time limits each day that are comfortable for the students. Some activities may take several days.

To "Lesson" Your Burden:

Crack Those Limits
Discuss what creativity is and how new ideas are born.

Encourage students to tell different ways in which creative thinking can help you when you have a problem to solve. Then work through the activities as a class or in groups of three or four.

A Welcome Change
Encourage students to discuss how they feel about changes they have seen or experienced. Discuss why some people dislike change and how this attitude affects the solving of problems. Do each activity as a class or in groups.

Discussion Ideas for Lesson Review:

These discussions are to be used after the activities to review and reinforce the techniques.

Crack Those Limits
Discuss with students how they might change or improve the ways they are presently doing things. Maintain an open-minded atmosphere so that students can share the ideas they create.

A Welcome Change
Encourage students to tell about emotions they have felt when faced with a problem. Ask them to tell why they may think that some things can't be changed. Discuss the idea that unless something is creating a problem, it may not have to be changed.

Crack Those Limits

Thinking about common things in uncommon ways helps us keep our minds open.

Good Problem-Solvers
Approach Problems
With Open Minds.

Think of a **common** ordinary school day in your life.

Do some **uncommon** thinking about that day. For example, imagine that the events of the day happen completely out of their usual order. What might your day be like?

First—**Think** of all the unusual things that might happen.
Second—**Record** ALL your ideas on a separate piece of paper.
Third—Meet with a partner and **share** your ideas with each other.
Fourth—**Select** your partner's most uncommon ideas.

Now think about some **common** things that have to be done as a part of living. Think about making a bed and everything you must do to get the job done.

Meet with a partner. Together think **uncommon** thoughts. List all the new and better ways you can think of to make a bed. ACCEPT ALL IDEAS!

After listing your ideas, go back and put a ✓ in front of any unusual ways you thought of.

PATH TO ACTION:
Choose a job you have to do that you really dislike. Then think of all the better ways you could do the job and still do it well.

Put all your ideas on paper **without judging**.

After ALL ideas are recorded, put a ✓ in front of all the unusual ideas on your list.

Be ready to explain your most unusual ideas to the class.

A Welcome Change

Change is a part of growing and living every day of our lives.

*To Be a Good Problem-
Solver, Accept Change
As a CHALLENGE
Instead of Blindly
Fighting It and Looking
For Someone to Blame.*

Think carefully as you answer the following questions.

Let your ideas flow...

1. What changes happen in your life?

2. What major changes have you seen since you were born?

3. What would you like to be able to change?

Some problems are hard to change. The job of bringing about changes may seem too difficult.

DO NOT BE DISCOURAGED! People **can** change things **if** they are active and creative. See what you can do with the problems below. Write your ideas for change in the second column. Put a ✓ in the third column if you believe this problem is too hard to change.

IDEA	I might begin to change this by...	This problem is too hard to change.
1. Pollution of the Earth		
2. Unwanted Pets		
3. People Blaming Others for Their Problems		
4. Dishonesty in the World		

PATH TO ACTION:
Meet with a small group. Choose a recorder. Let each member of the group tell the recorder which of the problems in the chart he or she felt could be changed by some action.

Have the members of the group take turns telling their most unusual ideas for bringing about some change for each problem.

PREPARE

Base Camp Set-Ups

Prepare for Problem Solving

Teacher's Trail

Base Camp Set-Ups

Preparing to Identify the REAL Problem:

To prepare for isolating and identifying the basic problem, the problem-solver must 1) collect information and 2) discover the important (basic) parts of the problem.

Suggested Teaching Routes:

1. Problems that are real to students often involve them negatively and emotionally. By using **safe** problems, students learn the techniques of problem solving so that they may then use those techniques to solve their own problems.

2. Students will need time and help with the skills of research for the these fact-finding activities.

To "Lesson" Your Burden:

Capture the Facts
This activity may be done by presenting each step ORALLY so that you can reassure students that they **are** able to use their imagination.

Mind Those Facts
Because a pantomine is required, this is a good team activity.

File the Facts
Using pictures or the real object increases the number of ideas.

Discussion Ideas for Lesson Review:

These discussions are to be used after the activities to review and reinforce the techniques.

Capture the Facts
Discuss the ways in which keen observation adds to one's knowledge. Elicit that to be creative, one must have facts on which to build new ideas.

Mind Those Facts
Have students think of some ancient object and predict how that object might be used by people in the year 2035. Discuss why objects or ideas are discarded as *old* instead of being used in new ways.

File the Facts
Encourage students to share their ideas. Have them discuss how listing attributes helped them get new and unexpected ideas.

Capture the Facts

If you are a sharp observer, you can use the facts you know to create NEW ideas.

Those Who Solve
Problems Know Where
To Find the Facts
And How to Use Them.

Use your **knowledge** and **imagination** as you follow the suggestions below:

1. **Think** of any object.
2. **Visualize** the object in your mind. (Really SEE it. Look at each part. Notice its characteristics—how it feels, sounds, and smells. Look for any unusual features it may have.)
3. **List** all the characteristics of your object on a separate piece of paper.
4. **Look** at a door. Use the facts you listed about your object to give you some ideas about ways to change the door. You may take the door apart or remove anything you want (in your mind!) as you figure out how to add characteristics to the door.

Now **talk** to another person about the ideas that came to you when you combined the facts on your list with a door.

Design your new door on a separate piece of paper.

Add labels and details to make your ideas clear and complete.

Find a way to **share** your design with the class.

BASE CAMP SET-UPS:

Follow these suggestions to help you use known FACTS to create new ideas:

1. On a separate piece of paper name all of the **different sources** of information about countries or states.
2. Choose a country or a state and write its name on your paper.
3. Use as many sources of information as you can to find out what your chosen country or state has a lot of (for example, sand, money, trees, people). List the things under the name of the state or country.
4. Now use your IMAGINATION to create different ways to use the things your place has too much of. Your ideas or inventions must **benefit** people.
5. Create a design or model of your favorite idea and to explain it to the class.

Mind Those Facts

Put your knowledge (or what you understand from your past experience) together in different ways. Hunt for new relationships between different facts. The more "connections" you can make between what you know and what you imagine, the more new and unusual ideas you will have.

Problem-Solvers Know How to Spark New Ideas by Putting Unrelated Facts Together.

Think of a styrofoam cup.

List all the characteristics of that cup on a separate piece of paper.

Imagine that you are a person in an early Indian tribe. In what ways might you use the styrofoam cup. List all of your ideas on a sheet of paper.

Meet with others in a small group. Select the most unusual idea, the one thought of by the fewest number of people.

Plan a pantomime to show how the cup could be used by the imaginative Indian from ancient times.

Present the pantomime to the class. Have them guess how the cup is being used.

BASE CAMP SET-UPS:
You are traveling with an archaeologist and you discover this strange artifact while digging.

No one seems to be sure about its use or purpose.

Think of as many uses for it in today's world as you can. Write them down.

Now write down the possible uses that its owners might have had for it in ancient times.

Pick an unusual use to share with the class. See if you were the only one to have that idea.

File The Facts

Organizing and classifying facts can lead to new ideas when those facts are combined in unusual ways.

The Lowly Jobs Of Sorting and Filing Facts Can Be Used to Get New Ideas.

In the chart below, familiar objects are listed in the first column. Think of each object as you consider the following:

1. What shapes can be seen in the object?
2. What are the main parts of the object?
3. What are **all** the actions the moving parts make to get the job done?

Complete the following chart by putting as many facts as you can in each space.

OBJECT	SHAPES	MAIN PARTS	ACTIONS
Bicycle			
Vacuum Cleaner			
Scissors			

Choose ONE IDEA FROM EACH COLUMN. Put the three ideas on a new sheet of paper.

Let these ideas simmer and churn in your mental blender.

Put the three facts together in different ways and see what new ideas come to mind.

Then jot down all the new ideas you can create from thinking about these three facts.

DO NOT JUDGE ANY IDEA YET!

BASE CAMP SET-UPS:

Try the same steps with three different choices of ideas.

When you hit upon an exciting new idea that might lead to some new process or invention, TAKE THE TIME to develop the new idea by drawing it or explaining it to others.

HONEY
IDENTIFY

Discoverer's Outlook

Identify the *Real* Problem

Teacher's Trail

Discoverer's Outlook

Identifying the REAL Problem:

Students must guard against rushing to find solutions. They must conscientiously stay with a problem situation until they can understand it and accurately **identify the main problem.**

Suggested Teaching Routes:

1. The expression "murky muddle" refers to a vague situation needing redefinition as a problem.
2. The teacher should use discretion in deciding whether students work alone or together.
3. Various recorders should be selected for different team activities.

To "Lesson" Your Burden:

Capitalize on the Unexpected
Although the teams are given similar situations, the results will vary greatly. Allow several days to thoroughly work on each problem.

Clear the Way to the Real Problem
The beginning stages of problem identification are presented. Using a team approach will help make clearing the "murky muddle" easier. Allow a lot of time for this activity.

Use a "Not" Remover
This activity is difficult for some children. A team approach may be necessary.

"Bare" the Details
Explain each step of problem identification. Allow teams to work slowly together.

Become a Perfect Shot
Students use the statement from the previous activity to help them accurately state the total elements of the **real** problem. Statements may vary among teams. Have students brainstorm many synonyms for verbs such as make, create, and find. Ask them to choose a verb that is ACTIVE and GENERAL enough to encourage many solutions.

Clear Away the "Murk"
Provide students with copies of this diagram before they begin the activities in this section.

Discussion Ideas for Lesson Review:

These discussions are to be used after the activities to review and reinforce the techniques.

Capitalize on the Unexpected
Encourage students to share their ideas. Have them discuss how listing attributes helped them get new and unexpected ideas.

Clear the Way to the Real Problem
Let each team present their *real* problem orally. Discuss the different problems that are shared and why there is a variety in them. Assure students that it is fine to have different problems identified as long as they are related to the "murky muddle."

Use a "Not" Remover / Become a Perfect Shot
Give students a lot of time to discuss their reactions to this complicated process. Ask them if they have observed anyone who makes decisions using this process. Have them give examples of times when the "wrong" problem may have been solved. Let them use this process on other "murky muddles" so they are able to use it more easily.

Clear Away the "Murk"
Students should keep this chart to help them through the steps of problem identification.

Capitalize On The Unexpected

The unexpected—even unexpected mistakes—can lead to exciting discoveries.

Allowing a PREPARED MIND and CHANCE To Work Together Is a Good Way to Ignite Ideas.*

Do this activity in teams of three. Each team will need a recorder to jot down ideas.

Directions for each group:

1. **Select** one of the groups of animals below:

A	B	C	D
goldfish chicken gopher	dog lizard giraffe	seahorse cat elephant	chimpanzee camel spider

2. **Think** of all you know about each animal in the group you selected.
3. Have the recorder **list** everything you know about each animal.
4. Use the characteristics that you list to help you think of **new ideas** for the problems below. Have the recorder list all ideas for each.

Problem I:
Suppose you could not reach the top shelf of a cupboard. Which animal characteristics might you use to create new ways to solve this problem?

Problem II:
Suppose your alarm clock were broken. Which animal characteristics might you use to inspire new ways to be awakened in the morning?

Problem III:
Suppose you wanted to design an underwater home of the future. What animal characteristics might you use to think of ways to design that home?

DISCOVERER'S OUTLOOK:

Let the recorder read aloud each problem and all the ideas your team had for solving it. Decide which ideas are the most unusual for each problem.

Choose the problem which has the **greatest number** of unusual ideas.

Put these unusual ideas together to create an invention which will solve the problem you chose.

Plan a presentation to your class explaining why they need your new invention.

* A prepared mind is one which is full of facts and memories.

Clear the Way To the Real Problem

Being a good problem-solver means that you take time to figure out the real problem. Problems usually come to use as "murky muddles." It is up to us to change a "murky muddle" into a clear, specific problem so that we can begin working on it.

Creative Problem-Solvers Keep Asking, "What Are ALL the Possible Problems?" As They Explore A Predicament.

Read the following "murky muddle":

GASOLINE COSTS TOO MUCH

Change this "murky muddle" into the REAL problem by following these steps:

Step 1—On a separate piece of paper write ALL the problems that might be caused by gasoline costing too much.

Step 2—Decide which problems on your list are the most important. Put a ✓ in front of any problem that...

- keeps people from getting things done
- makes people feel unhappy or discouraged
- affects people's way of life

Step 3—Let the check marks help you decide which problem is the most important one to solve.

Step 4—Write the real problem on the lines below.

The real problem is ______________________________

____

____

DISCOVERER'S OUTLOOK:

Think of some problem you have in your life. Quickly jot it down.

Follow the four steps described above. Use your own criteria to find the most important problem in Step 2.

The real problem is ______________________________

____

____

Use a NOT-REMOVER

Negative statements can interfere with the clear understanding of a problem.

*The Wise Seeker-After-
The-Real-Problem
Accentuates
The Positive.*

See if you can avoid tying yourself up in knots as you work on the following "murky muddle":

WE HAVE AN ENERGY CRISIS

On a separate piece of paper record ALL the possible problems that might be caused by an energy crisis.

"NOT-REMOVER" SYSTEM:

1. Put a ✓ in front of any statement you listed which contains a "NOT." ("Nots" are statements that contain negative words such as NO, NOT, NO one, CAN'T, WON'T, AREN'T, or might NOT.)

2. **Read** the first statement you checked. **Think** to yourself: Why is this a problem?

   SAMPLE: People CAN'T go away on vacations. Why is this a problem?
   1. People will have to learn from books instead of going places.
   2. Motels might go out of business.
   3. People will get crabby.

3. Reread the first statement you checked and write the **reasons why** it might be a problem. Use a new sheet of paper. BE SURE TO AVOID ANY "NOT" STATEMENTS!

4. Now follow steps one through three for any other "Not" statements in your list. Remember, *naughty* statements containing *nots* may *knot* up a precise understanding of the real problem!

5. Read all the positive statements regarding the "murky muddle" that you have written.

6. Decide which problem is the most important and crucial to people as they deal with the energy crisis. Share your idea with the class.

DISCOVERER'S OUTLOOK:
From now on, if you accidentally make a "NOT" statement for a possible problem, follow this formula:

Step 1—Ask yourself this question: Why might it be a problem if. . . ? (End the question by filling in your "not" statement).

Step 2—Then list all the positive answers to this new questions you can think of.

"Bare" the Details

A "murky muddle" holds the secret to the REAL problem. As we think about all the problems in it, we must collect enough DETAILS to really understand the problem.

Attending to All the Details Is a Secret of Success in Identifying The Real Problem.

Discover all the ways you can collect DETAILS in order to clear a "murky muddle":

PEOPLE WATCH TOO MUCH TELEVISION

Step 1—Collect **details** by searching your memory for all the ways that television affects people. Record all your ideas on paper without judging them.

Step 2—Examine the details of the "murky muddle" by thinking about these questions:

Who might be involved in this "murky muddle"? (Many may be involved.)

What possible problems **might** the "murky muddle" cause? (Avoid the "NOTS.")

Why might this "murky muddle" cause problems?

When might this "murky muddle" cause problems? (Now? Next year? Ten years from now? Next century?)

Where might this "murky muddle" cause some problems? (At home? At school? In a city? In a country? Throughout the world?)

These questions will help you think of a greater variety of possible problems in order to find the REAL problem.

Step 3—Record all the possible problems you thought of by doing Step 2.

Step 4—Take time out to **gather information** about the "murky muddle." **Research** the facts and write them down. **Sort out** the facts that apply to the "murky muddle."

Step 5—Go over the steps above and add any **new possible problems** that you can think of to your list.

DISCOVERER'S OUTLOOK:

You now have a long list of details that show many problems resulting from the fact that people watch too much television. Right?

To help you find a REAL problem to write on the lines below, put a **P** by any ideas on your list that affect a lot of people; an **F** by any ideas that affect the future of our nation; and an **M** by those ideas that have the most to do with the "murky muddle."

Look at the idea(s) marked with these letters. If you have several ideas, combine them into one problem statement. Write your problem statement on the lines below.

The real problem is ______________________________
(who) (do what)

____
(why) (where) (when)

Become a Perfect Shot

Doing something about the problem is the next step. Effective problem-solvers often state the problem as a question to help them take creative action to solve it.

Creative Problem-Solvers Know How to State the Problem to Stir the Mind to Dynamic Action.

Write the problem statement from the end of the previous activity here:

____

____

Change your problem statement into a creative question. Begin with these words:

How might __________________________________
(who?) (do what?)

____
(why?) (where?)

____
(when?)

The verb you use in your problem statement can make the problem easier to solve.

Example: How might we MAKE people watch less television every day in their homes so that the family will talk to each other more?

It is hard to MAKE people to do anything. Try the following verbs as replacements for "make": encourage, interest, educate, and help. See how the problem changes with different verbs.

Now **think** of all the verbs you could put in your problem statement and record them.

Discuss with your team how the verb changes the problem.

Select a verb for your problem statement that . . .

- will help you think of the most ideas.
- will encourage a great variety of possible solutions.

Write your **perfect** problem statement here: ____________________

____

____

DISCOVERER'S OUTLOOK:
Think of all the possible solutions to the problem above. Be sure to record all ideas. Did your "perfect statement" help you think of more solutions? __________

Clear Away the Murk

Murky Muddle

INVENT!

Inventive Leap

Creative Ideas for Alternative Solutions

Teacher's Trail

Inventive Leap

Creating Unique Alternative Solutions:

The common way to solve a problem is to quickly try out ideas that pop into the mind. Creative problem-solvers try to generate quantities of solutions, some of which may seem "strange" or "way out." This often leads to the creation of unique, inventive solutions.

Suggested Teaching Routes:

1. Point out that the applicable technique or quality of creative thinking is at the top of each page.
2. Memories are tricky and ideas are easily lost. Be sure the ideas are always recorded in some way.
3. Vary the times allowed according to the complexity and pace of the activity.
4. Create a **safe** classroom environment where ideas can be shared without fear of ridicule or failure.

To "Lesson" Your Burden:

Let the Ideas Pour
Work in pairs on the INVENTIVE LEAP section.

"Can" the Critic
Discuss the illustration and talk about critical attitudes and comments that can destroy creative thinking. Organize the class into groups and encourage them to become supportive of each other by orally discussing the CLIMB rules. (Duplicate and distribute CLIMB rules found on page 61.)

Spring-Fresh Ideas
Allow students ten minutes for each activity to determine how **fluent** their thinking is.

Learn to Leap
Encourage students to realize that a flexible thinker manipulates around limitations. Do not let them add new situations or objects, but encourage them to use the examples in "Let Loose an Avalanche of Ideas" to stretch ideas. Prepare 5" x 8" cards or paper for the INVENTIVE LEAP.

Create Hot Ideas from Many Sources
Allow students ten minutes to create their ideas. Help them use the symbols to evaluate their ideas.

Keep the "Image" in Imagination
Discuss whether students have noticed differences between they way they visualize a book and the way the movie version pictures it. Talk about how the ability to picture a book in their minds helps them enjoy reading.

Read each situation slowly, pausing at the dots (. . .) to allow students time to visualize the story.

Imagination Frees Ideas
Curiosity and imagination take TIME. Allow for a relaxed, calm atmosphere during these activities.

Free Those Funnybones
This activity is fine for a group or team. Be sure students use CLIMB rules.

Think Links
Remind students to use CLIMB rules to help create many ideas. Review the method of attribute listing.

Pause to Reflect
Review with the students some of the techniques they have used to create ideas. Discuss the fact that ideas sometimes come to people when they are doing something else. Compare the process to the hibernation of bears to help students understand the process.

Point to a Decision / Develop Clear Solutions
Discuss the need to set standards before making decisions or judgments. Allow a lot of time.

Discussion Ideas for Lesson Review:

These discussions are to be used after the activities to review and reinforce the techniques.

Let the Ideas Pour

Give students opportunities to name the attributes of common objects. Then encourage them to consider the attributes of an event, concept, or idea to solve problems creatively in social studies, science, or language arts.

"Can" the Critic

Discuss with students the situations in which *they* have judged too soon. Let them also tell about the times they *have been judged* too quickly. Set up a non-judgmental atmosphere in the classroom in which students practice problem-solving by brainstorming, using the rules for withholding judgment. (Refer to this page whenever the critics agitate.)

Let Loose an Avalanche of Ideas / Spring-Fresh Ideas

After students have evaluated their **fluency**, discuss the results of their findings. Ask them to evaluate whether or not they found themselves judging themselves too soon. Remind them of how premature judging can stop ideas.

Take Advantage of "Failure"

Ask students to present their findings about "failure" to the class. Discuss the fact that "failure" may be used to defeat a person only if that person is not flexible enough to try *another* way.

Learn to Leap / Create Hot Ideas from Many Sources

Discuss with students all the reasons why *flexible thinking* increases activity. Then brainstorm the ways each person might remain a flexible thinker while working on problems.

Keep the "Image" in Imagination / Imagination Frees Ideas

Encourage students to discuss how vivid their images were. Discuss how much color, details, and movement they were able to picture. Provide many opportunities for students to create visual images to enhance their intuition and creativity.

Everything Can Be Related / An Extraordinary Stretch

Ask students how they felt as they combined unlike objects. Explain to them that creative people use this method to create new inventions. Give them opportunities to continue putting together unlike things.

Free Those Funnybones

Allow students to have a *safe* time for creating "opposite" or "strange" ideas. The ideas may seem "silly" at first, but they *will* become possibilities.

Think Links

Discuss with students the purpose of taking things apart in our minds and putting them back together in new ways. Explain how this process helps us to see ordinary things in unusual ways.

Pause to Reflect

Ask students to tell whether they had any new ideas *spring* out of their minds (Aha!) when they practiced "creative hibernation." Let them tell all the reasons why they think this happens to people.

Point to a Decision

Discuss with students the difficulty and time this activity took to complete. Ask them to think of ways they could use this method daily so that it would become easier for them.

Develop Clear Solutions

It is essential to review as many parts of creative problem solving as possible. The major examples in this activity should be used as a basis for review. It is helpful for students to retain copies of this page for use as a reference when solving a problem.

Let the Ideas Pour

One way to make ideas flow is to list an object's attributes in an organized way.

Creative Problem-Solvers
Pour out Many Ideas
From Their Memory
When They Are Needed.

Select any object from your desk or from what you are wearing. It can be large or small, but you should be able to **touch** it.

Now study the chart on the following page. Use the ideas that are "pouring" out of the five water lines to help you think of all you know about your chosen object.

Write down your ideas on a separate sheet of paper. Be sure to list **all** your ideas.

How many attributes did you list? _____

INVENTIVE LEAP:

Try to think of ways to make a stapler trouble free and easy to use.

List the attributes of a stapler. Use all five of the ideas for attribute listing described in this activity to help you.

Beside each attribute write a way to **improve** or **change** it.

Choose the new attributes that might make the stapler more trouble free.

Plan how you will present your new ideas to another person.

After both partners have shared ideas, select those ideas that have inventive possibilities.

Design a stapler of the future with your inventive ideas.

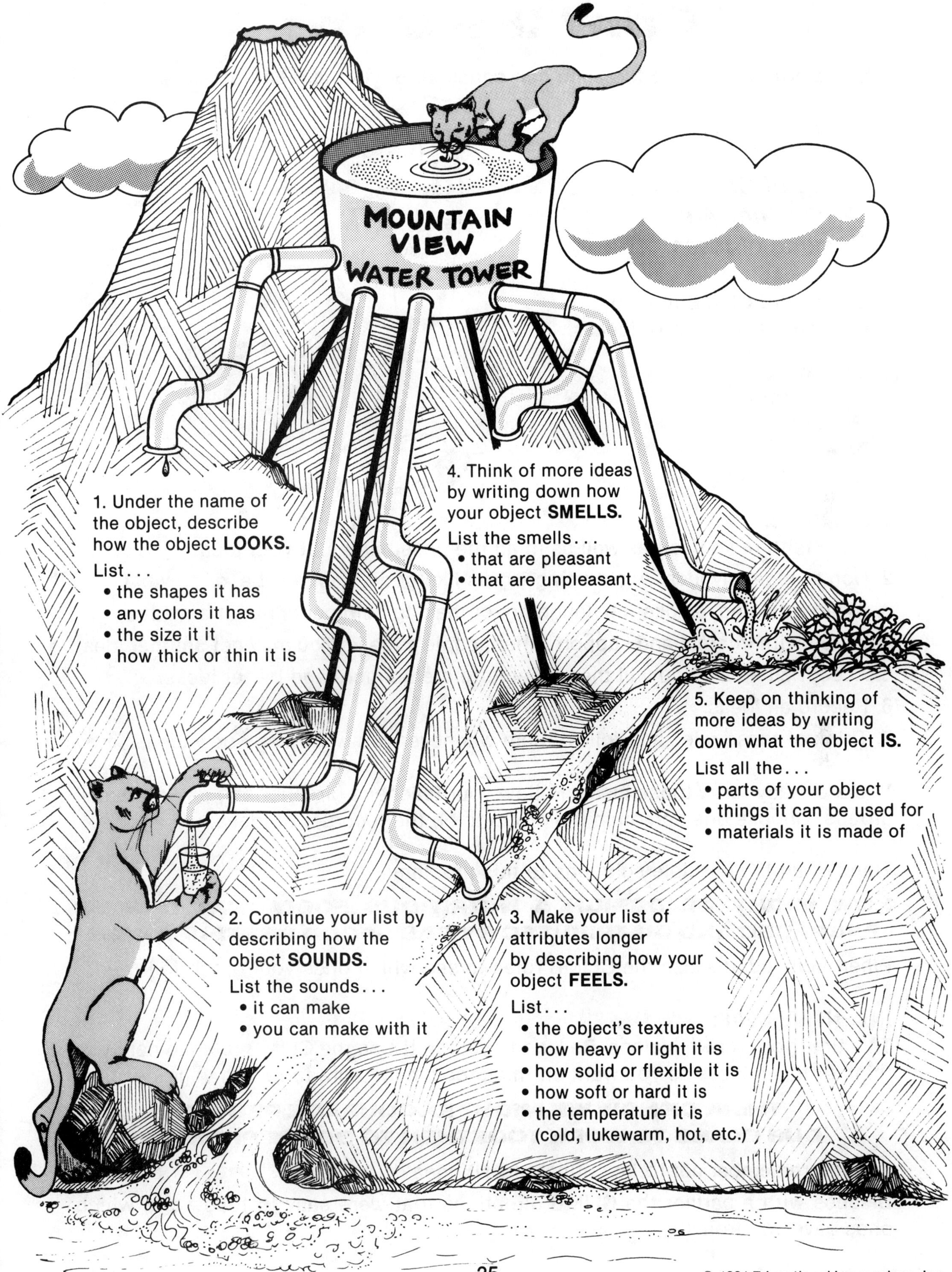
MOUNTAIN VIEW WATER TOWER
1. Under the name of the object, describe how the object **LOOKS.**
List . . .
• the shapes it has
• any colors it has
• the size it it
• how thick or thin it is
2. Continue your list by describing how the object **SOUNDS.**
List the sounds . . .
• it can make
• you can make with it
3. Make your list of attributes longer by describing how your object **FEELS.**
List . . .
• the object's textures
• how heavy or light it is
• how solid or flexible it is
• how soft or hard it is
• the temperature it is (cold, lukewarm, hot, etc.)
4. Think of more ideas by writing down how your object **SMELLS.**
List the smells . . .
• that are pleasant
• that are unpleasant.
5. Keep on thinking of more ideas by writing down what the object **IS.**
List all the . . .
• parts of your object
• things it can be used for
• materials it is made of

"Can" the Critic

Being critical of ideas too soon can cause all of your ideas to disappear.

Inventive People
DELIBERATELY Stop
Thinking of Criticisms
While They Are
Thinking of Ideas.

Use the word CLIMB to help you stimulate the flow of ideas.

C **reating**
L **imitless**
I **deas**
M **eans**
B **rainstorming**

Climb Rules:

1. Have faith in yourself as well as in all the possibilities of your ideas.
2. Don't judge any idea. Avoid using words like good, bad, maybe, or so what.
3. Avoid frowning, snickering, laughing, or making comments about any idea.
4. Listen with interest and support other people's ideas. You may get **another** idea!
5. Accept all ideas. You will then be able to create more and better ideas.
6. Record all ideas.
7. Think of these rules and follow them whenever you want many new ideas.

You are ready to try these ideas. Follow your teacher's directions to get into small groups. Choose one person in the group to be the recorder of ideas.

Think of **all** the possible solutions to this problem:

HOW MIGHT WE DESIGN A NUTRITIOUS FOOD THAT CAN BE PREPARED AND DISTRIBUTED BY FAST-FOOD RESTAURANTS?

When finished, discuss the CLIMB rules to see which ones your group followed.

INVENTIVE LEAP:
This time you will work alone. Be kind to yourself! Use the CLIMB rules to help you think of many ideas as you work on this problem (be sure to record your ideas):

THINK OF HOW WE MIGHT ENCOURAGE PEOPLE IN OUR CLASS TO WORK TOGETHER TO SOLVE PROBLEMS.

Did you remember not to be critical of ANY idea?

Discuss with a partner the CLIMB directions that were easy to follow and which ones gave you trouble.

Let Loose
An Avalanche of Ideas

An inventive creator of solutions is able to "can the critic" and let the ideas roll out. Fluency is important when thinking of possible problems or solutions. Your best ideas may come after you have had many ideas.

Problem-Solvers Know That the MORE Ideas You Have, the BETTER They Seem to Get.

Work with a partner on these problems. Remember to record ALL ideas. Follow the CLIMB rules to think of as many solutions to this problem as you can.

WE HAVE DEPENDED FOR A LONG TIME ON ERASERS TO ELIMINATE OUR MISTAKES.

Think of all the things that are wrong with erasers (any kind) at the present time.

Now try to **think** of possible solutions to THIS problem:

HOW MIGHT WE CONVENIENTLY AND CAREFULLY ELIMINATE (not erase) ERRORS WE MAKE ON PAPERS IN SCHOOL OR IN BUSINESS?

Remember, use CLIMB to record as many ideas as you can!

When you finish recording your ideas, COUNT how many possible solutions you and your partner created for the problem statement. Record the total at the top of your paper. (This is your FLUENCY score.)

Continue to use fluent thinking as you face ANY problem.

INVENTIVE LEAP:
Work with a group of two or three people to solve this problem:

HOW MIGHT WE RECORD ALL OUR IDEAS WHEN WORKING IN A GROUP SO THAT ALL MEMBERS OF THE GROUP CAN SEE THE LIST OF IDEAS THEY ARE WORKING ON?

Choose a recorder. Be as FLUENT as you can and be sure to CLIMB!

Then select the ideas you think might help to solve the problem.

The next time your group is recording ideas, use the ideas you thought of during this activity and see how your solutions work.

Spring-Fresh Ideas

Fluent thinkers can pull ideas out of their minds WHENEVER they need them.

Practicing Fluency Brings Confidence That New Ideas Will Always Be There to Spring Forth When Needed.

Try this activity by yourself to see how fluent you are becoming.

Challenge 1

On the next page you will find the number 5 written ten times, scattered in different places around the sheet. **Think** of ALL the possible things you might make out of the 5's by adding any lines or details that you want.

Create as many ideas around the 5's as you can in ten minutes.

Challenge 2

On a piece of lined paper, list all the ideas for the problem below. You will be given ten minutes to do this.

SUPPOSE YOU GOT UP ONE SATURDAY AND NONE OF YOUR FRIENDS WERE HOME. THINK OF ALL THE WAYS YOU MIGHT ENTERTAIN YOURSELF WHILE SPENDING ALL DAY SATURDAY ALONE.

INVENTIVE LEAP:

How fluent is your mind at creating ideas? What helps you become a more fluent thinker?

It is important for you to have answers to these questions if you are to be a roaring success as a problem-solver.

Evaluate yourself by completing the following questions:

1. How many ideas did you create by using the 5's? ____________
2. How many ideas did you think of for spending a Saturday alone? ____________
3. Did you get more ideas when creating pictures or when creating words? Are the two scores the same? ____________
4. Use the above information to decide whether you are more creative with words or with pictures. What did you decide? ____________
5. Did you remember to use the CLIMB rules to help you? ____________

Take Advantage of "Failure"

Just because an idea fails to work in one situation, that doesn't mean that it won't work in another one. By thinking of different ways to use an idea that has "failed," you may create something you never thought of before.

Inventive People Use "Failure" to Spring To New Ideas.

Suppose you designed a portable ENLARGER like the one below.

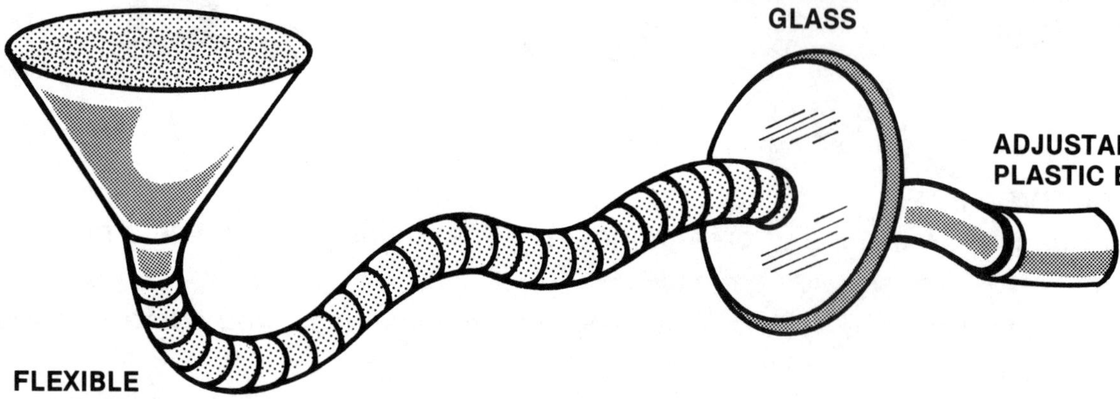

Dimensions:
Length = 8 inches
Height = 3 inches

However, when you tried it out, you discovered that the enlarger was a "failure"; it did not work.

Some people might throw away this idea, but here is a way to use "failure" to create more ideas!

Think of ALL the new ideas or inventions you can create by using the following kinds of FLEXIBLE THINKING. Put your ideas on a separate piece of paper.

1. Imagine the enlarger to be as **LARGE** as a classroom and think of all the new things it might be. Record your ideas. Use the CLIMB rules to be fluent.
2. Visualize the enlarger to be as **SMALL** as a fingernail. Record all the things it might then become.
3. "Doodle" on scratch paper and **REARRANGE** the parts of the enlarger by changing their order or by moving them in various directions. Record all the new inventions you think of.
4. Using the enlarger as a basic plan, **ADD** any lines or details that you wish or **COMBINE** the enlarger with other objects. Record all the ideas that these changes bring to your mind.
5. Instead of a plastic eyepiece, **SUBSTITUTE** a tape recorder. List all the new ways you can think of to use this device.
6. Take off or **ELIMINATE** any of the parts of the enlarger that you wish. Create new ways to use what is left of the enlarger. Record your ideas.

Now, **select** several of your new ideas that...

- benefit people
- might be possible to make and sell in the next 20 years

Finally, put the new ideas you selected together and **create new inventions** to present to the class.

INVENTIVE LEAP:
Select the name of one person listed below or think of another person you would like to know more about. Use books or interviews to discover WHEN that person turned "failure" into a new idea and HOW it was done.

Marie Curie
Thomas Edison
Alexander Fleming
Benjamin Franklin
Charles Goodyear
Abraham Lincoln

Learn to Leap

Inventive leaps are new ideas that come to use when we combine common objects or ideas in new ways in order to solve a problem.

Inventive Leaps Can Make Your Day When You Need New Ideas To Solve Problems.

Imagine yourself in each of the problem situations that are described below. Think of the object(s) you might use in a new way to solve each problem you face. Then explain HOW you might use the object(s) to solve the problem.

Problem Situation 1

You are riding your bike on a deserted country road. Being very thirsty, you decide to take a drink from your thermos. As you try to unscrew the lid, you find that it won't turn. You try tapping it gently, but it won't budge and you are getting even more thirsty. You look in your backpack and discover that you have a transistor radio, a tuna sandwich, a plastic spoon, a fishing line, and a sweater.

Which OBJECTS would you use to remove the lid safely?

____

HOW would you use the objects to solve this problem?

____

____

Problem Situation 2

You have survived a plane crash and are lost alone in a mountain area. You are afraid that you might starve before finding your way out of the mountains. You have with you a handkerchief, a rubber band, a comb, and a pencil.

Which OBJECTS could you combine to get some food?

____

HOW would you use them to solve your food problem?

____

____

INVENTIVE LEAP:
During the next week, keep track of any times you are inventive and use FLEXIBLE THINKING. Set up a 5" x 8" card or paper as shown below:

INVENTIVE RECORD

Date   Flexible Thinking Ideas

Record any examples of your use of flexible thinking to accomplish something or to solve a problem. At the end of a week, meet with a partner to share your ideas.

Create Hot Ideas From Many Sources

Flexible thinkers take many different approaches to problems.

Creative Problem-Solvers Use Flexible Thinking to Come Up with MANY Possible Solutions.

See how FLEXIBLE your thinking has become. Think of as many DIFFERENT solutions to the following problem statement as you can in ten minutes. Record your ideas WITHOUT JUDGING so that you can be as fluent as possible.

HOW MIGHT WE DESIGN SAFE AND ECONOMICAL WAYS TO KEEP PEOPLE WARM ENOUGH DURING THE WINTER?

To check how creative your thinking is, judge your ideas by the following standards:

FLUENCY: Count the total number of ideas and put the number at the top of your paper. If you had 25 or more ideas, you are a fluent thinker.

FLEXIBILITY: Read each idea and evaluate it by using the following symbols. Next to each idea, draw the symbols that apply.

- > — Any idea that can keep a LOT of people warm.
- < — Any idea that is SMALL enough to be handy to use.
- ◇ — Any idea that ADDS TO or COMBINES with something we use now.
- ⟠ — Any idea that uses COMMON OBJECTS of today in NEW or DIFFERENT ways.
- ○ — Any idea that uses the PARTS of different objects to create a new way to keep people warm.
- □ — Any idea that IMPROVES a common idea or object to make it a better way to keep people warm.
- △ — Any idea that ELIMINATES the present ways of keeping warm and creates totally NEW ways of maintaining warmth in people.

Now count each DIFFERENT symbol you have used in judging your ideas. This will be your FLEXIBILITY score. Seven points is the highest possible score. If you had five or more points, consider your thinking FLEXIBLE.

INVENTIVE LEAP:
Use the ideas you have thought of to design on paper a NEW way to keep people warm. Put in all the details you can think of to make your design complete. Then add any labels you need to make your design understandable.

Keep the "Image" In Imagination

Many people lose the ability to see pictures in their heads as they rely more and more on movies and television to create pictures for them.

Perfect Problem-Solvers Easily Create Fantastic New Ideas from the Visions and Pictures They Keep Running Through Their Minds.

Check to see if your mind can create good mental images as you listen to your teacher tell the following situations. Take time to SEE each picture in detail in your head as you listen.

(Note: the 3 dots (. . .) indicate a pause in the reading to give students time to "see.")

Visualization 1

You are in a land beyond time. . . Rising out of the ground near your feet are tiny blades of glass. . . Watch the blades slowly grow taller. . . and taller. . . They grow up all around you. . . They begin to sway. . . Watch them move slowly. . . upward. . . back and forth. . . See them glisten and shine as light catches their movement. . . Look at them begin to turn and spiral. . . See them twist. . . Then watch them untwist. . . Watch crystals form along each glass blade. . . See crystals run like raindrops down each glass blade. . . Look at the red, blue, and yellow lights reflected from the crystals as they slide down the blades and fall to the ground. . . You watch each crystal sink slowly into the spongy ground surface. . . You hear a whirring sound. . . Look up and see all the glass blades swaying and twisting. . . Watch them as they slowly drill their way back into the ground. . . See them disappear a few at a time. . . Look at the ground and watch the last glass blade sink below the surface.

Visualization

2

In your mind, select a color from your box of crayons... Imagine that you scribble that color heavily on a piece of blank paper...See that color lift off the paper...Make it take the shape of a colored cloud...See that cloud move out the door...Have it travel to a large white wall...Make the cloud burst against the wall...Watch the color drip down the wall...Have a large bird drink the color as it drips...Watch the bird turn the color of the dripping goo...Make the bird fly off into the sky...As the bird flies, let the sky in the bird's path turn the same color as the bird...Keep the bird flying...Watch all light disappear...See the bird disappear...Watch the sky turn black...Feel how soft and warm the black sky is...Wrap it around you...Pull the black sky away from you...Roll it into a ball...Mold it into the shape of a stick...Make the stick small enough to fit into your crayon box...Turn the stick into a black crayon...Put it in your crayon box.

INVENTIVE LEAP:

Take time to create your own set of changing images. Choose any object or situation. Mentally create changes in it. Do it SLOWLY. Make one change at a time. Try to make your mental pictures VIVID and COLORFUL.

As your imaging improves, you may begin to feel that you are a part of your pictures.

Imagination Frees Ideas

Curious people allow their minds to "play" with strange and unusual ideas. The more we let curiosity set our imaginations free, the more original our ideas become.

Curiosity Is an Important Key to Imagination and Imagination Is an Important Key to Problem Solving.

Let your curiosity guide you as you "play" with these ideas on blank pieces of paper. Withhold any comments or judgments.

IMAGINATION INSIGHTS

Image 1

Draw a building of any size or shape. Imagine a monkey's tail and draw it anywhere on the building. Think of a leaf of any size or shape. Draw it anywhere on the building. Visualize a spoon of any size or shape and draw it anywhere on the building.

Now turn your drawing around and look at it from several directions. Allow your imagination to soar by trying to see new pictures or ideas. Keep thinking of new things as you turn your picture to look at it.

Then add lines, color, and details to create a new and imaginative product for the future.

Image 2

Draw a front view of a face LIGHTLY on your paper. Imagine what objects might look like a nose. Erase the nose and draw in an unusual object.

Imagine any objects that look like a mouth. Substitute any object you want and draw it in place of the mouth.

Use your imagination to substitute objects for the eyes, the ears, the hair, and the eyebrows.

Let your feelings and imagination work together by adding anything else your intuition or hunches help you to create.

When you are finished, be **courageous** enough to explain your creation to another person.

INVENTIVE LEAP:

Einstein said, "Imagination is more important than knowledge." Major breakthroughs in science and invention come when **imagination** and **intuition** are allowed to grow into possibilities.

Look carefully at any object in your classroom or at home.

Draw the object and its details lightly on a piece of paper.

Then **substitute** other objects which have similar characteristics for the the details you drew lightly on your paper. Let your ideas become "strange" or different as you use your imagination.

Follow your imagination and work on "new" objects several times a week.

Everything Can Be Related

Any two things you can think of can be related. Connecting in an imaginative way the attributes of one thing to the those of another can spark original ideas.

Successful Problem-Solvers Risk Stretching Their Imaginations to Make "Impossible" Ideas Possible.

Anything is possible! Try using **connections** while working with this problem:

HOW MIGHT WE KEEP TRAFFIC MOVING SMOOTHLY AND SAFELY ON OUR HIGHWAY SYSTEMS TO ELIMINATE TRAFFIC JAMS AND TO SAVE FUEL?

Consider the **main** parts of the toaster and **how the parts function** to do their jobs.

1. How is the bread put into the toaster? ______________________

2. How is the bread held by the toaster? ______________________

3. How is the bread lowered into the toaster? ______________________

4. Why is lowering the bread important to the operation of the toaster? ______________________

5. How does the toaster know how long to toast? ______________________

6. What does the toaster do to the bread when it is finished? ______________________

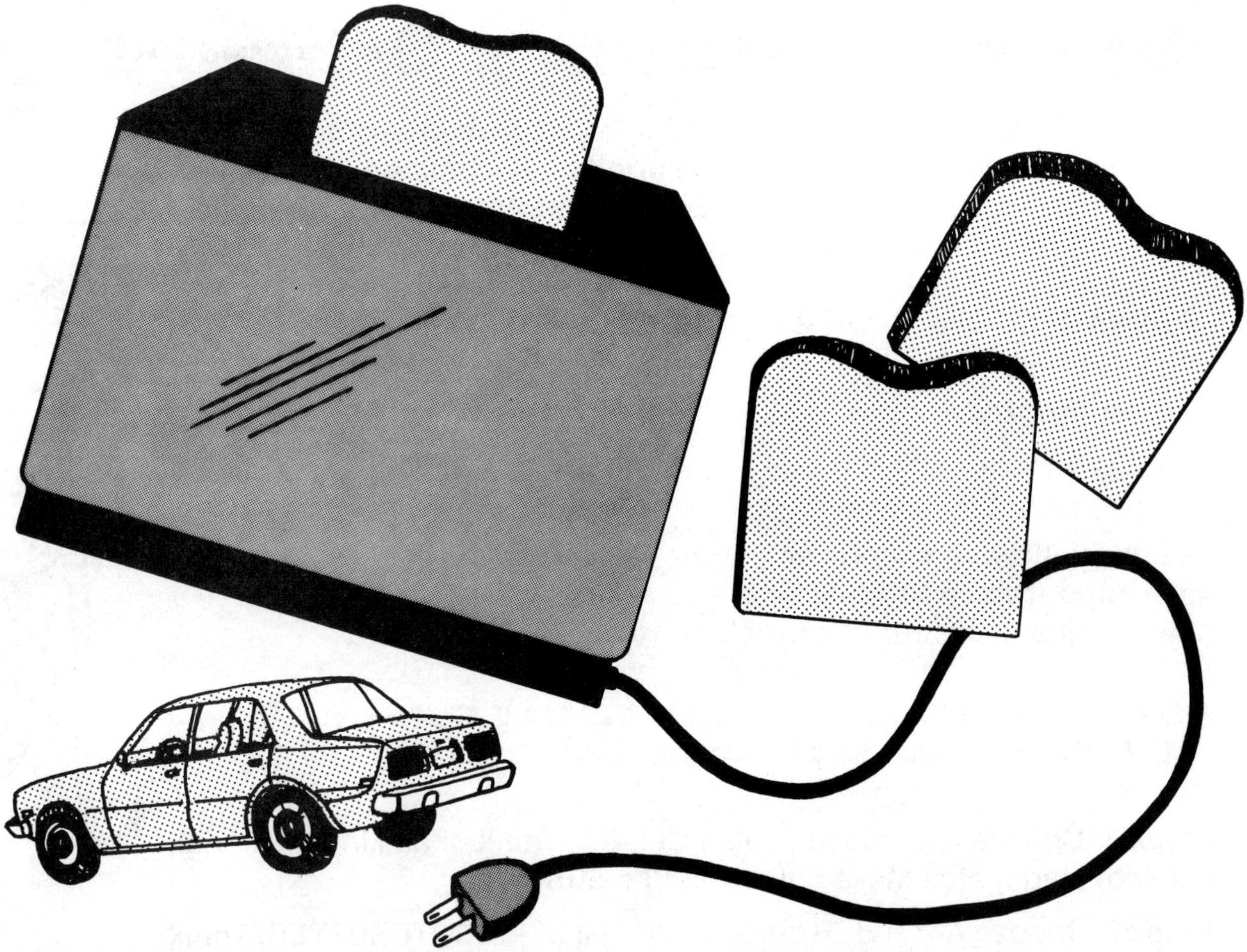

Now ask yourself, "How might I use the ideas about the toaster to think of efficient ways to keep traffic moving?" The following ideas will give you a start:

Idea 1: **Visualize** in your mind what might happen if you SUBSTITUTED cars for the bread.

Idea 2: **Visualize** what might happen if you SUBSTITUTED a traffic system for the toaster.

Many ideas should POP up!

Use the CLIMB rules and imagination to think of many possible solutions to solve the traffic problem above.

INVENTIVE LEAP:

Now think of any object other than a toaster. Think of ITS parts and functions. Record your ideas.

Relate the main parts and the functions of this object to the traffic problem in order to think of new possible solutions. Add these ideas to the list of ideas you got when you related the toaster to the problem.

When you have twenty or more ideas, select the solutions that would be the safest and that would save the most fuel.

Explain your new solution to another person in your class.

An Extraordinary S-t-r-e-t-c-h

Creative problem-solvers stretch their creative ability by finding ways to invent original, uncommon ideas. One way to succeed at inventing original ideas is to relate familiar objects in different, unusual ways.

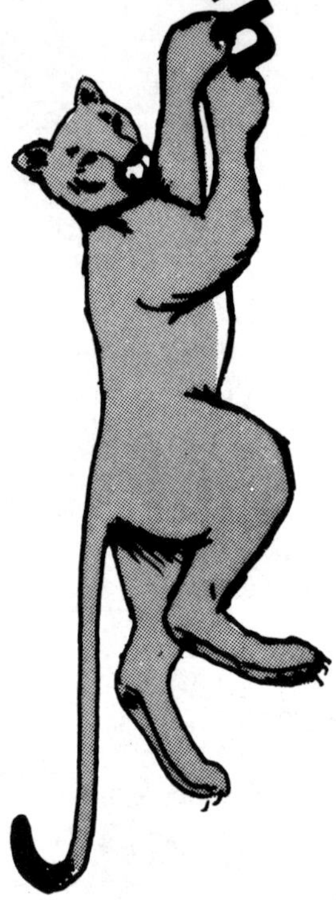

People Who Want to Be Creative Problem-Solvers Regularly Invent Uncommon Ideas.

Use the following experiment to set your mind free and to help you find new, original ideas for this problem:

HOW MIGHT WE OBTAIN A THREE-DAY SUPPLY OF GROCERIES WITHOUT LEAVING HOME?

Step #1: **Choose** ANY object. (Try a CLOCK. Think of all kinds—digital, cuckoo, alarm, etc.) Make a list of all its attributes.

Step #2: **Choose** ANOTHER object. (Try a jar of PEANUT BUTTER. Think of all kinds—chunky, smooth, etc.) Make a list of all its attributes.

Forget the clock and the peanut butter. They were only to give you ideas! Re-do steps one and two using objects of your own choosing.

Step #3: **Select** one attribute from each of your two new lists.

Step #4: **Combine** the two attributes any way you can to create possible solutions to the grocery problem. ("Play" with the two attributes and stretch the ideas to fit the problem. DO NOT JUDGE!)

Step #5: **Record** your possible new solutions on a piece of paper.

Step #6: **Select** two more attributes and think of additional possible solutions. **Add** them to your list of possible solutions.

Step #7: Continue to **combine** attributes from each list until you have eight or more possible solutions.

Step #8: **Judge** which possible solutions would be the most convenient and efficient for people to use.

INVENTIVE LEAP:
When you are trying to solve a problem, learn to use the ordinary to create extraordinary solutions. Try the system above to seek solutions to this problem:

HOW MIGHT WE PROVIDE PEOPLE WITH SAFE AND CONVENIENT WAYS TO VISIT PLACES OF INTEREST IN THE WORLD?

Free Those Funny Bones

Use the funny ideas that may pop into your head while you are trying to think of unique, original ideas. These funny thoughts may become a future possibility for a person with VISION.

A Sense of Humor Helps People Create Unique Ideas

Have fun as you deliberately try to use humor to help you find original ideas.

Imagine what some of the advertised products on the market might be like if they did the OPPOSITE of what they were supposed to do!

Enjoy thinking of the possibilities of the following new products:

TRID SOAP: This soap leaves a layer of dirt when it is used.

RODO DEODORANT: This product creates a strong odor when it is used.

RELLAMS PLANT FOOD: When plants are fed this food, they become smaller.

YAD-ETIN LIGHT BULBS: These light bulbs turn daylight into darkness.

Think of **who** might use each of these products and what they could be used for. **Record** ALL the ways each product might be useful or beneficial to people.

TAKE THE RISK OF HAVING SOME SILLY IDEAS!

INVENTIVE LEAP:
Ask the recorder to read the ideas your group had for the use of **one** new product.

Choose any ideas that sound silly or funny.

Discuss ways you might change those ideas into possible future products.

Use the CLIMB rules to think of as many new products as you can that do just the OPPOSITE of what they are supposed to do. Record all your new product ideas.

Have your team select the one or two new products from your list that it judges will benefit people the most and/or may have the possibility for use in the future.

Design and label how the product(s) will work.

Explain all the possible benefits of the product.

Give your new product a name.

Present your new product and its benefits to the class in a creative, convincing way.

Think Links

One way to brush up on your ability to create original ideas is to use the parts of the problem itself to help you.

The Parts of a Problem Can Be Used to Inspire New Solutions.

Here's a formula to help you use the parts of a problem to solve that problem:

Step #1: Think of ALL the parts of your problem. Write them down.

Step #2: Choose one or two of those parts to work with.

Step #3: List the major attributes of each part you've chosen.

Step #4: Make several changes in each attribute.

Step #5: Combine the changed attributes in different ways.

Step #6: Presto! Great, original ideas begin to smile through to you.

Try the formula on the following problem:

HOW MIGHT WE KEEP OUR TEETH CLEAN DAILY TO ELIMINATE PLAQUE AND DECAY?

List all the parts (things) involved in this problem. (Your list may include dental floss, toothbrush, toothpaste, mouthwash, diet, etc.)

Choose **toothpaste** and **toothbrush** as the parts of the problem you will work with.

Use the chart on the following page to give you a better idea of how the process works. Think hard to include ALL the main parts of the toothbrush and toothpaste.

Follow the directions given at the top of each column and change each part that you listed in the MAIN PARTS column.

CHANGES IN THE ATTRIBUTES

MAIN PARTS: Toothbrush & Toothpaste (In Any Order)	Make Heavier Or Lighter	Make Larger Or Smaller	Change The Shape	Change What It Is Made Of	Substitute Something Else To Do The Job
Bristles					
Tube					
Flavor					

When you have completed the chart, **combine** all of your ideas in the ways suggested below to create new solutions to the teeth-cleaning problem.

1. Take one idea from each column (in any order) and write them on a piece of paper.
2. Work the ideas around and use them to think of possible solutions to the teeth-cleaning problem.
3. Again choose an idea from each column and use all of them to create additional possible solutions to the problem.
4. Keep selecting ideas from the different columns to create MANY NEW WAYS to keep our teeth clean.
5. Be sure to RECORD all ideas!
6. Share your new ways to clean teeth with a class member.

INVENTIVE LEAP:
Think of something you have to take care of or be responsible for. Use the steps above to think of inventive new ways to solve the problem.

Pause to Reflect

Sometimes people get frustrated while trying to solve a problem. When this happens, a good problem-solver realizes that it is time to do some "creative hibernation*." The mind is then free to let unique ideas spring up.

Taking time for "Creative Hibernation" Frees the Mind to Think of Unique Possible Solutions.

Form a team to work on the problem below. Be sure to try "creative hibernation" as a part of what you do to find a solution to the problem.

HOW MIGHT WE PRESERVE THE NATURAL BEAUTY OF OUR COUNTRY WHILE WE UNCOVER THE ENERGY SUPPLY WE WILL NEED DURING THE NEXT TEN YEARS?

1. Let each member of your team collect information about alternative sources of natural energy.

   Where are they to be found?

   How do they affect the land or the people's environment?

2. Each team member should present any findings to the group for information and discussion.

3. The team should use the CLIMB rules to list ALL the possible solutions to the problem.

4. The team should make another list of ALL the ways things have been preserved in the past. (Drying, freezing, canning, etc.)

5. Team members should use their imaginations to apply these ways of preserving things to the problem above. (The recorder should add any new solutions to the list compiled in number 3.)

*Creative hibernation is letting a problem "rest" in the caverns of your mind while you attend to other things. This time of backing-off releases frustration and allows any creative new idea to BOUND out of your mind.

6. Team members should now try to visualize some funny pictures in their minds:

Think of an oil rig pumping UP the ground into hills.

Think of a coal mine adding earth and plants to the areas around it.

Tell about one or two funny pictures that come to mind as you think about energy.

7. Now it's time to try "creative hibernation." STOP HERE until tomorrow to give team members time to "doodle" their ideas on paper or to talk to other people. Remember to write down any ideas that come to you during this period.

8. SPRING TIME! When the team meets the next day, let the new and unusual solutions "spring out" of each member. Be sure they are recorded! Your team now has a great supply of possible solutions to the problem.

9. Evaluate the possible solutions as your recorder reads them aloud.

Put a plus (+) by any solutions that you think might be major breakthroughs.

Share your best creative solutions with the class.

INVENTIVE LEAP:
Use this same approach to work on a problem affecting your class or school.

Point to a Decision

After withholding judgment to create more unusual ideas, the possible solutions must be judged to find out which solution is the most appropriate.

An Important Part of Problem-Solving Is Knowing When to Withhold Judgment And When to Use It.

Use the Creative Problem Solving steps described in the previous activity to think of all the possible solutions to the following problem:

HOW MIGHT WE DEVELOP CLOTHING THAT WILL BE LONG-LASTING AND COMFORTABLE TO WEAR IN THE FUTURE?

Record all ideas WITHOUT JUDGING.

Now it is TIME TO JUDGE! But it is important to set **criteria**, or standards, before choosing the most **appropriate** solutions.

1. Discuss USEFUL criteria by using the following ideas:

   A. Does the criterion (standard) consider people and how the possible solution BENEFITS PEOPLE?

   B. Does the criterion consider whether the solution SOLVES THE PROBLEM WITHOUT CAUSING POSSIBLE NEW PROBLEMS?

   C. Does the criterion consider whether the solution is POSSIBLE TO CARRY OUT USING OUR PRESENT KNOWLEDGE AND TOOLS?

   D. Does the criterion consider whether the SOLUTION IS WORTH THE COST to the **betterment** of our lives?

   E. Does the criterion consider whether the SOLUTION IS WORTH THE TIME AND EFFORT needed to carry it out?

   F. Does the criterion consider whether THE SOLUTION CAN BE EASILY UNDERSTOOD AND USED by the people involved?

   G. Does the criterion consider whether people will be able to ACCEPT AND VALUE the solution?

2. Think of ALL the criteria needed by your team to judge the solutions to the clothing problem. Be sure these criteria are recorded on a separate piece of paper.

3. Use the chart* to help you choose a solution to the problem.

A. Select ten possible solutions to the clothing problem and put the **main idea** for each one on the chart.

B. List the five **most appropriate** criteria to use for judging the solutions.

Criterion 1: ______________________________

Criterion 2: ______________________________

Criterion 3: ______________________________

Criterion 4: ______________________________

Criterion 5: ______________________________

NOTE: The five criteria listed on the chart below will **stand for** the five criteria you have just listed above.

C. Use CRITERION 1 to rank the listed solutions from 10 to 1. A **10** means that the solution fits the criterion the **best.** A **1** means that the solution fits the criterion the **least**. Use a ranking number only once. DISCUSS EACH SOLUTION CAREFULLY BEFORE JUDGING!

D. Do the same for each criterion until the solutions have been ranked according to all five criteria. Remember to discuss each solution before judging.

	CRITERIA RANKING SYSTEM					
POSSIBLE SOLUTIONS (Main Idea)	Criterion 1	Criterion 2	Criterion 3	Criterion 4	Criterion 5	TOTAL POINTS
1.						
2.						
3.						
4.						
5.						
6.						
7.						
8.						
9.						
10.						

E. For each solution add **across** the chart and record the total number of points received in the column marked TOTAL POINTS. Read the solution receiving the most points. AT LAST, A DECISION! Write it in the space below.

____

____

*Based on the works of Sidney J. Parnes and E. Paul Torrance

Develop Clear Solutions

Creating and choosing a solution to a problem is an important beginning. The ability to improve and develop the solution is necessary to help it succeed.

Thoughtful Problem-Solvers Accept the Challenge of Improving the Chosen Solution

1. **Discuss** with your team members the ways you might IMPROVE your chosen solution to the clothing problem from the previous activity:

    Add other ideas (or possible solutions) to it.

    Substitute different ideas to make the solution better.

    Eliminate any unnecessary parts of the solution.

    Imagine combining the solution with new ideas.

    Make the solution more **complex** or **detailed.**

    Simplify unimportant parts of your solution.

2. **Record** any ideas for improvement of the solution. Evaluate the improvements by using the ideas from the previous activity. **Select** the improvements to be used.

3. Let some team members create various designs to include with the new ideas for the solution. Have other members plan how the solution might be put into effect.

    Think of the people, places and objects involved with carrying out the solution.

    Think of all the **possible problems** you may run into when using this solution.

4. Meet as a team and discuss the designs and the plans that the members created.

5. Combine the parts of the designs and plans that your team judges to be the **most effective** for your solution.

6. Plan a presentation of the completed solution to the class.

7. Judge whether the solutions are well planned and well presented.

INVENTIVE LEAP:
You are now ready to solve ANY PROBLEM! Use the problem solving chart, CLIMB rules, creative hibernation, and evaluation by criteria to remind you what to do.

CLIMB

Use the word CLIMB to help you stimulate the flow of ideas.

C reating
L imitless
I deas
M eans
B rainstorming

Climb Rules:

1. Have faith in yourself as well as in all the possibilities of your ideas.
2. Don't judge any idea. Avoid using words like good, bad, maybe, or so what.
3. Avoid frowning, snickering, laughing, or making comments about any idea.
4. Listen with interest and support other people's ideas. You may get **another** idea!
5. Accept all ideas. You will then be able to create more and better ideas.
6. Record all ideas.

Think of these rules and follow them whenever you want many new ideas.

ACT

Mountain "Do" Cliffhangers

Implement Creative Solutions

ACT

Teacher's Trail

Mountain "Do" Cliffhangers

Implementing Creative Solutions:

It is essential that students understand the importance of acting on or carrying out their solutions. To **resolve** a problem requires organization, planning, and the acceptance from others of the final solution.

Suggested Teaching Routes:

1. Use the chart on the following two pages FIRST to review the steps of creative problem solving.

Encourage students to use the chart as they work on a "murky muddle" which the class has identified.

Give them time to understand the process and to ask questions.

2. The team approach greatly helps to spur the group members on to action.

To "Lesson" Your Burden:

Problem-Solving Chart
Help the teams by using an "easy" problem of their choice. If the "murky muddle" deals with objects or things, it is easier to work with.

Present the sections one at a time to guide the teams slowly.

If necessary, review the "Clear the Murk" Problem Solving Chart, the Climb rules, the rules for establishing criteria by which to judge solutions, and ways to improve solutions.

Give Solutions Intensive Care
Use teams for this activity. Allow students to use plenty of scratch paper for creating details and planning.

It Will Never Work
Help students create a stapled packet or use a spiral notebook in which to record their surveys. Allow a week or more for the surveys to be completed.

Be Convincing
Discuss with students the things that give them confidence. Ask them to think of ways to build their confidence when they are presenting new solutions to problems. Some of these ideas can then be used as class rules to maintain a creative atmosphere.

Discussion Ideas for Lesson Review:

These discussions are to be used after the activities to review and reinforce the techniques.

Problem-Solving Chart
Give students time to evaluate how much the chart helped them as they solved the "easy" problem. Encourage them to add words or notes to the chart to help them. Since this chart will be theirs to keep, encourage them to use it on any problem they may have.

Give Solutions Intensive Care
Give students opportunities to tell **how** they planned their solutions. Explain that planning in detail for all the possibilities they can think of helps make a solution successful. Have students use these steps in planning events in their lives.

It Will Never Work / Be Convincing
Ask students to continue to observe the ways people are influenced to do things. Encourage students to select various ways to present their solutions effectively.

Forge... Climb... Leap... to the Peak of Problem Solving!

PREPARE TO UNDERSTAND THE PROBLEM

- Gather the facts
- Use the facts to find more facts
- Understand the facts
- Sort, file, and combine the facts

IDENTIFY THE PROBLEM

Use the unexpected to help you see a problem in a new way.

Take TIME...
...to search for the REAL problem
...to remove "NOTS"
...to take care of details
...to tell who, what, where, when and why
...to find the best verb

STEP UP TO ACTION

Accept challenge
Keep an open mind

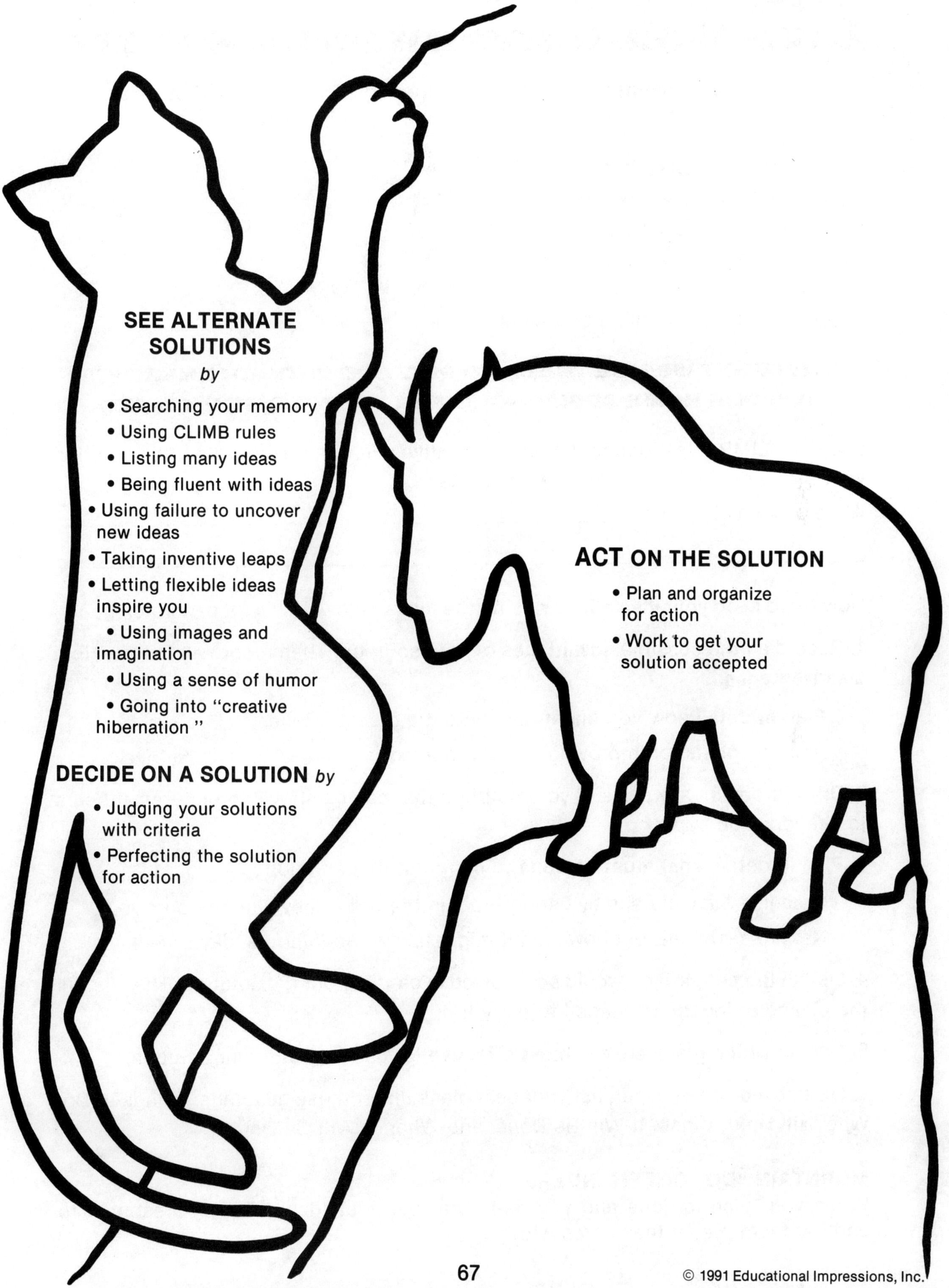
SEE ALTERNATE SOLUTIONS
by
• Searching your memory
• Using CLIMB rules
• Listing many ideas
• Being fluent with ideas
• Using failure to uncover new ideas
• Taking inventive leaps
• Letting flexible ideas inspire you
• Using images and imagination
• Using a sense of humor
• Going into "creative hibernation"
DECIDE ON A SOLUTION by
• Judging your solutions with criteria
• Perfecting the solution for action
ACT ON THE SOLUTION
• Plan and organize for action
• Work to get your solution accepted

Give Solutions Intensive Care

Ideas can disappear quickly if they are neglected. An idea that gets somewhere is one that is well planned with many details.

People with Creative Solutions Must Work on Their Ideas to Keep Them Alive and Growing.

Suppose you were working on this problem:

HOW MIGHT WE USE TRASH TO PROVIDE ENOUGH ENERGY TO RUN OUR HOME APPLIANCES FOR THE NEXT TEN YEARS?

Use the CLIMB rules to record many alternative solutions. Then select the solution your group decides is the most appropriate.

Write your solution here. ____

____

Now try to **keep your idea alive** by using the plans below. Use a lot of scratch paper.

1. Record all the possible **advantages** of your solution. Then record all the possible **disadvantages.**

   Plan in detail how you might eliminate the disadvantages.

   Add any plans for improving the advantages.

2. Draw or design any parts of your solution that can be shown in pictures. It helps to **see** ideas on paper.

3. Plan in detail **what must be done** to carry out this solution.

   Organize these details by listing them in the order they will be done.

   Next to each idea, put how long it might take to do it (hours, days, weeks, etc.).

4. List **all the people** who would be involved in carrying out the solution. Then list **all the places or locations** needed to carry it out.

5. Decide **which plans** are the **most effective** for carrying out your solution.

6. On a new piece of paper, list your best plans under these headings: Things to Do, Who Will Do It, Where It Will Be Done, and When It Will Be Done.

MOUNTAIN "DO" CLIFFHANGERS

When your plan is done and you feel **sure that your idea will live**, present it to another team. See if they agree with you.

It Will Never Work

No matter how GREAT an idea or solution may be, it takes the support and understanding of PEOPLE if it is to take root and grow.

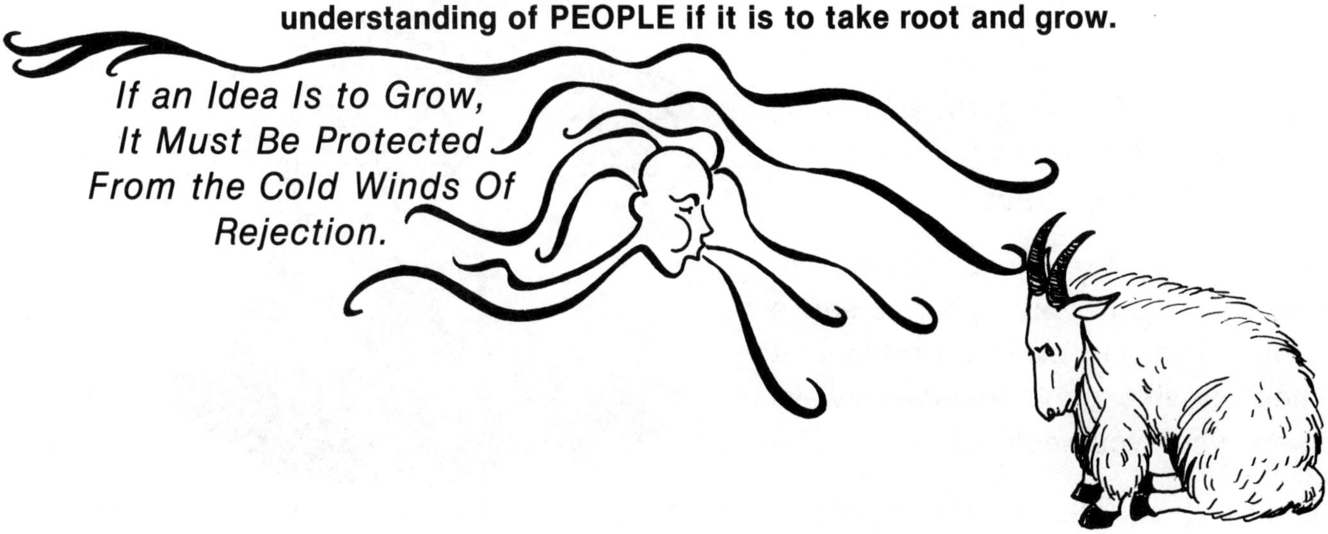

Many people RESIST a new idea or solution simply because it brings a CHANGE. Try these ideas to help you CONVINCE PEOPLE that they need to try your idea.

Idea 1

Discuss with your team all the NEGATIVE THINGS you have heard people say about NEW ideas or solutions.

Use the CLIMB rules to think of all the ways you might deal with these attitudes so that people might listen to new ideas BEFORE judging them.

Record ALL ideas. Store them in a safe place.

Idea 2

OBSERVE and STUDY the ways professional advertisers overcome people's resistance to trying new things. How do they CONVINCE PEOPLE that they need their product?

Watch television commercials or listen to radio advertising. Look for **propaganda techniques** that. . .

- get people to use products.
- get people to help causes (such as the Heart Fund, United Way, etc.)

Collect newspaper and magazine advertisements, announcements, and brochures that appeal to you.

Idea 3

INTERVIEW people to find out why they accept a product.

List the things people SAY THEY DO before accepting a new idea.

List all the different ways, besides using the product, that encourage people to accept a product.

MOUNTAIN "DO" CLIFFHANGERS

Organize your team so that each person can report his or her findings to the group.

Based on the facts collected, use CLIMB to add new ideas to your list of ways to deal with attitudes from the IDEA 1 section.

Be Convincing

If you believe in yourself and in your ideas, other people will believe in you too.

Successful Problem-Resolvers Are Organized And Confident Of Their Ideas

A good way to build confidence in yourself is to use your creative problem-solving skills so often that they are like good friends—always there when you need them.

Meet with your team and use your creative problem-solving skills to IDENTIFY and SOLVE the following "murky muddle."

> The geological history of the continent of Antarctica is being studied by scientific teams from several countries. The scientists are also interested in locating natural resources to be removed and used by people in the future. Each country has its base camp in a different area of the continent. All the countries are trying to claim the areas where they are camped. Disagreements have begun about who should own and control Antarctica. There is also some concern about damage to the land and wildlife if this continent is developed for its resources.

Begin discussing this "muddle" with your team.

Work through the problem-solving process to your most appropriate solution.

- Plan your solution in detail. Make it ready to put into ACTION.
- Follow this **acceptance route** to convince others of the value of your solution.
  - Decide as a team which methods you will use to get people interested in your solution.
  - Plan how you will communicate your solution to people.
    - What will you say? (Use simple, clear words. Find an interesting way to explain your solution.)
    - What VISUAL method will you use? (Use diagrams, skits, and commercial techniques.)
  - Get organized! Be sure everyone has a job to do. Decide on the order of the presentations.

MOUNTAIN "DO" CLIFFHANGERS

NOW actually make an INTERESTING PRESENTATION to your class.

After you finish, ask class members to tell you the good points about your presentation and to suggest ways you might have improved it.

THE PEAK OF PROBLEM SOLVING

The following examples of "murky muddles" may be used with students one "murky muddle" at a time. Teams should be formed and directed to use the creative-problem-solving process. They should have their Creative-Problem-Solving Chart and their CLIMB chart to help them.

Problems of Today

The lunch period in many schools allows time to take a break from school as well as to eat. Sometimes, if the weather is poor or if there is nothing to do, the time allotted for lunch seems to be too long. Some people think that there might be a better way to use the lunch time. Identify the real problem and find an effective solution by following the steps of creative-problem-solving.

Some people like to listen to modern music when they are working as well as when they have free time; however, other people may not like the music or may think it is too loud. Sometimes disagreements occur and special rules have to be set up. There might be a way that people who enjoy music can listen to recordings or the radio without disturbing others. Identify the real problem and seek many alternative solutions as you creatively try to solve the problem.

Liquids in cups, glasses, or other containers may be easily spilled by children and adults alike. Once soft drink cans or bottles are opened, we must be careful not to tip or drop them. Any sudden or careless move can knock over a cup or glass and spill the contents. There are better ways to store and serve liquids if you use the steps of creative-problem-solving to work on the problem.

The amount of land on the earth has remained basically the same while the number of people has grown rapidly. The earth is becoming overcrowded and eventually there may not be enough food or land for all the people living on our planet. Isolate the real problem and seek a solution to the problem using creative-problem-solving.

Along most roads and freeways advertisers have put up large billboards and signs. These advertisements are great for business, but they sometimes hide beautiful scenery or make the roadway look cluttered. Creative problem-solvers should work on ways that might make the environment more attractive, but would allow businesses to advertise. Find the real problem and work to solve it in a creative way.

Problems of Tomorrow

The large oil, coal, and power utility companies have well-trained people and complicated equipment to search for and develop new sources of energy. In the future, solar or hydrogen power might be developed so that everyone could have free energy to use whenever it was needed. BUT, if the new energy developed by the large companies were free and easy-to-get, these companies might hurt their own business; in fact, they might go out of business altogether. This could hurt our economy. Carefully identify the real problem. Then use the creative-problem-solving process to find a solution.

Within 200 years, daily trips into outer space may become common. It may be possible to spend vacations on various planets or even in the outer regions of the universe. Think of the possible problems that might develop from constant space travel and then use creative-problem-solving to identify and solve the real problem.

As people change and develop greater awareness, their senses may become more sensitive and acute. Our sense of hearing may become as sharp as a dog's. Human eyes may become adapted for seeing in the dark. Our sense of touch may allow people to sense vibrations and temperatures to a greater extent. Taste and smell may be intensified. Think of some problems this greater sensitivity might cause. Locate the real problem and creatively take steps to solve it.

Computers are being used for more and more tasks every day. In the future, computers may manage our time, our environments, and our work. Think of some of the problems the reliance on computers might cause. Use creative-problem-solving to isolate the real problem and to create an effective solution to the problem.

As a team, think of as many possible problems for the future as you can. Record these problems and store them in a safe place. Your teacher will give you time to work on each problem—IN THE FUTURE.